Debbie Bliss
Home

Debbie Bliss
Home

27 hand knits for living

Trafalgar Square Publishing

DEDICATION

To the memory of Tommie

First published in the United States of America in 2005
by Trafalgar Square Publishing
North Pomfret, Vermont 05053

Printed and bound in Singapore by Tien Wah Press

1 3 5 7 9 10 8 6 4 2

First published by Ebury Press
Random House, 20 Vauxhall Bridge Road, London SW1V 2SA

Library of Congress Control Number: 2005925891

ISBN-13: 978-1-57076-303-8
ISBN-10: 1-57076-303-8

Editor: Emma Callery
Designer: Christine Wood
Photographer: Pia Tryde
Stylist: Julia Bird
Pattern checker: Rosy Tucker
Charts: Anthony Duke

contents

Introduction 6 ♥ Knitting essentials 8

introduction

Debbie Bliss Home is a celebration of the art of homemaking. Whether you spend time in a stylish loft apartment, a country abode, or a waterfront beach house, making decorative or practical hand knits creates an individual and personal touch that makes your house a home.

To reflect our different lifestyles, the projects are divided into three sections: *Urban*, *Modern Country*, and *Seaside*.

The projects in *Urban* are worked in strong, graphic colors and with geometric shapes and spot patterns that sing out against the pared-down shapes and style of the contemporary house. A spotted bedspread or cushions in clashing shades will add a vibrant note to any room and a lime felted bag and colorful gloves are the perfect accessories to enliven a drab day in town.

Modern Country reflects the rural landscape with contemporary knits worked in natural yarns in russets, taupes, and browns, including a soft seed stitch wrap to snuggle into and a cozy jacket. For new or basic knitters, there are easy starter projects, such as a garter stitch washcloth and seed stitch potholder.

In *Seaside*, the knits take on a nautical theme with floor cushions and throws for picnics on the beach or deck, worked in crisp cottons and using stitch patterns that evoke the classic fisherman's Guernseys. A ribbed, casual jacket and a simple sweater for a child are ideal for a relaxed vacation wardrobe.

The *Debbie Bliss Home* collection includes knits that cover a range of knitting skills, from very easy to projects for the more advanced knitter. Happy homemaking.

knitting essentials

following pattern instructions

Figures for larger sizes are given in parentheses ( ). Where only one figure appears, this applies to all sizes. Work the figures given in brackets [ ] the number of times stated afterward. Where 0 appears, no stitches or rows are worked for this size. As you follow the pattern, make sure that you are consistently using the right stitches for your size—it is only too easy to switch sizes inside the parentheses. One way to avoid this is to photocopy the instructions first and mark off the figures for the size you are knitting with a colored marker.

The quantities of yarn quoted in the instructions are based on the yarn used by the knitter for the original garment and amounts should therefore be considered approximate. A slight variation in gauge can make the difference between using less or more yarn than that stated in the pattern. Before buying the yarn for a garment, look at the measurements in the knitting patterns to decide which size you want to knit. Look at the actual finished measurements of the garment to make sure you are choosing the right size for you. The length of the garment is taken from the shoulder shaping to the cast-on edge.

gauge

Each pattern in the book gives a gauge—the number of stitches and rows per centimeter or inch that should be obtained with the given needles, yarn, and stitch pattern. Check your gauge carefully before starting work. A slight variation in gauge can spoil the look of a garment and alter the proportions that the designer wanted. A too loose gauge will produce uneven knitting and an unstable fabric that can droop or lose its shape after washing, while too tight a gauge can create a hard, unforgiving fabric.

To make a gauge square, use the same needles, yarn, and stitch pattern quoted in the gauge note in the pattern. Knit a sample at least 5in/12.5cm square. Smooth out the finished sample on a flat surface but do not stretch it. To check the stitch gauge, place a tape measure horizontally on the sample and mark 4in/10cm with pins. Count the number of stitches between pins. To check the row gauge, place the tape measure vertically on the sample and mark 4in/10cm. Count the number of rows between the pins. If the number of stitches and rows is greater than that stated in the pattern, try again using larger needles. If the number of stitches and rows is less, use smaller needles. If you are only able to obtain either the stitch or the row gauge, it is the stitch gauge that is the most important to get right, as the length of many patterns are calculated by measurement rather than the number of rows you need to work to achieve it.

garment care

Taking care of your hand knits is important. If you have invested all that time and labor into knitting them, you want them to look good for as long as possible.

Check the yarn label for washing instructions. Most yarns can now be machine washed on a delicate wool cycle. Prior to washing, make a note of the measurements of the garment or accessory, such as the width and length. After washing, lay the knitting flat and check the measurements again to see if they are the same. If not, smooth and pat it back into shape.

Some knitters prefer to hand wash their knits. Use detergent specially created for hand knits, and warm rather than hot water. Handle the knits gently in the water—do not rub or wring, as this can felt the fabric. Rinse well to get rid of any soap, and squeeze out excess water. You may need to get rid of more water by rolling the knitting in a towel, or use the delicate spin cycle of the washing machine. To dry the knitting, lay it out flat on a towel to absorb moisture, and smooth and pat it into shape. Do not dry knits near direct heat, such as a radiator. Store your knits loosely folded to allow the air to circulate.

needle conversion chart

This needle conversion chart covers all the knitting needle sizes used for the patterns in this book.

US sizes	UK metric	US sizes	UK metric
size 2	2¾mm	size 7	4½mm
size 2–3	3mm	size 8	5mm
size 3	3¼mm	size 9	5½mm
size 5	3¾mm	size 10½	6½–7mm
size 6	4mm	size 11	7½–8mm

standard abbreviations

alt = alternate

beg = beginning

cm = centimeters

cont = continue

dec = decreas(e)ing

foll = following

in = inches

inc = increas(e)ing

k = knit

kfb = k into front and back of next st

kfpb = knit into front and purl into back of next st to make one st

M1 = make one by picking up loop lying between st just worked and next st and working into the back of it

p = purl

patt = pattern

pfb = purl into front and back of next st

pfkb = purl into front and knit into back of next st to make one st

rem = remain(ing)

rep = repeat

skp = slip 1, knit 1, pass slipped stitch over

sl = slip

St st = stockinette stitch

st(s) = stitch(es)

tbl = through back of loop

tog = together

yo = yarn over

types of yarns

wool   Wool spun from the fleece of sheep is the yarn that is the most commonly associated with knitting. It has many excellent qualities, as it is durable, elastic, and warm in the winter. Wool yarn is particularly good for working color patterns, as the fibers adhere together and help prevent the gaps that can appear in Fair Isle or intarsia.

Some knitters find that a simple stitch such as seed stitch or garter stitch can look neater when worked in a wool rather than a cotton yarn.

cotton   Cotton yarn, made from a natural plant fiber, is an ideal all-seasons yarn, as it is warm in the winter and cool in the summer. I particularly love to work in cotton because it gives a clarity of stitch that shows up subtle stitch patterning, such as a seed stitch border on a collar or cuffs.

cotton and wool   Knitting in yarn that is a blend of wool and cotton is particularly good for children's wear. This is because the wool fibers give elasticity for comfort but, at the same time, the cotton content is perfect for children who find wool irritating against the skin.

cashmere   Cashmere is made from the underhair of a particular Asian goat. It is associated with the ultimate in luxury, and is unbelievably soft to the touch. If combined with merino wool and microfiber, as in my cashmerino yarn range, it is perfect for babies and children, as well as adults.

buying yarn   Always try to buy the yarn quoted in the knitting pattern. The designer will have created the design specifically with that yarn in mind, and a substitute may produce a garment that is different from the original. For instance, the design may rely for its appeal on a subtle stitch pattern that is lost when using a yarn of an inferior quality; or a synthetic when used to replace a natural yarn such as cotton will create a limp fabric and the crispness of the original design will be lost. We cannot accept responsibility for the finished product if any yarn other than the one specified is used. (See page 126 for yarn distributors.)

substituting yarns   If you do decide to use a substitute yarn, buy one that is the same weight and, where possible, has the same fiber content. It is essential to use a yarn that gives the same gauge as the original or the measurements will change. You should also check yardage or meterage—yarn that weighs the same may have

different lengths so you may need to buy more or less yarn. Check the yarn label. Most yarn labels now carry all the information you need about fiber content, washing instructions, weight, and yardage or meterage.

It is essential to check the dye lot number on the yarn label. Yarns are dyed in batches or lots, which can sometimes vary quite considerably. Your retailer may not have the same dye lot later on, so try and buy all your yarn for a project at the same time. If you know that sometimes you use more yarn than that quoted in the pattern, buy more. If it is not possible to buy the amount you need all in the same dye lot, work the borders or the lower edges in the odd one, since the color change is less likely to show there.

Debbie Bliss yarns

The following are descriptions of my yarns and a guide to their weights and types. Most of the yarns used in the designs are machine washable, but always check the yarn label for details. (See page 126 for yarn distributors.)

Debbie Bliss merino double knitting: a 100% merino wool in a double-knitting weight. Soft to the touch but hard-wearing. Approximately 120yd (110m)/50g ball.

Debbie Bliss merino aran: a 100% merino wool in an Aran or fisherman weight. Approximately 85yd (78m)/50g ball.

Debbie Bliss cashmerino aran: a 55% merino wool, 33% microfiber, 12% cashmere yarn in an Aran or fisherman weight. A luxurious yarn with a beautiful handle. Approximately 98yd (90m)/50g ball.

Debbie Bliss baby cashmerino: a 55% merino wool, 33% microfiber, 12% cashmere yarn in a sport weight. Approximately 91yd (84m)/50g ball.

Debbie Bliss cashmerino superchunky: a 55% merino, 33% microfiber, 12% cashmere yarn in a superbulky weight. Knits up quickly on larger needles. Approximately 82yd (75m)/50g ball.

Debbie Bliss cotton double knitting: a 100% pure cotton that knits up to slightly thicker than a standard double-knitting gauge. Approximately 91yd (84m)/50g ball.

Debbie Bliss cotton denim aran: knits to an Aran or fisherman weight. A soft and light, nonshrinking denim-look yarn. Approximately 74yd (68m)/50g ball.

Debbie Bliss alpaca silk: an 80% alpaca, 20% silk yarn that knits to an Aran weight. Approximately 72yd (65m)/50g ball.

Debbie Bliss maya or SoHo: a 100% handspun wool slub that knits up between an Aran and chunky weight. Approximately 137yd (126m)/100g hank for Maya and 72yd (65m)/50g ball for SoHo.

urban

humbug cushion

This is an unusual three-dimensional triangular cushion, which is firmly stuffed to

make it a great backrest. For a larger version, just add stitches and rows.

size
Approximate height 16½in/42cm.

materials
Six 50g balls of Debbie Bliss cotton dk in
Chocolate
Pair size 6 (4mm) knitting needles
17¾ x 33in/45 x 84cm17¾ x 33in of cotton
lining fabric
Styrofoam beads

gauge
19 sts and 28 rows to 4in/10cm square over
patt using size 6 (4mm) needles.

abbreviations
cm = centimeters
cont = continue
in = inches
k = knit
p = purl
patt = pattern
st(s) = stitch(es)

to make   With size 6 (4mm) needles, cast on 82 sts.
1st row (right side) K5, [p2, k5] to end.
2nd row Purl.
These 2 rows form the patt and are repeated throughout.
Cont in patt until work measures 32¼in/82cm, ending with a p row.
Bind off.

to make   With right sides together and taking ½in/1cm seams throughout, stitch together
lining   the short sides of the lining fabric to form a tube. Fold the tube flat with the
seam to one side and join from the seam to the fold at one end. Open out the
unstitched end and refold the fabric so the first seam lies centrally, and stitch the
seam, leaving 2in/5cm unstitched at one end. Turn right side out and fill with
Styrofoam beads. Stitch the opening closed.

to finish   Join cast-on and bound-off edges of knitted piece to form a tube. Fold the tube
flat with the seam to one side and join from the seam to the fold at one end.
Open out the unstitched end and insert the filled lining, then stitch the seam
closed so that the first seam lies centrally.

medium spot cushion

A large spot on a basic cushion makes a dramatically bold statement against a

neutral background.

size
Approximately 16in/45cm square.

materials
Four 50g balls of Debbie Bliss merino dk in
Chocolate and one 50g ball in Lime
Pair size 6 (4mm) knitting needles
16in/45cm square pillow form

gauge
22 sts and 30 rows to 4in/10cm square over
St st using size 6 (4mm) needles.

abbreviations
cm = centimeters
in = inches
k = knit
St st = stockinette stitch
st(s) = stitch(es)

note
When working motif, use separate balls of
yarn for each area of color and twist yarns
together on wrong side to avoid holes.

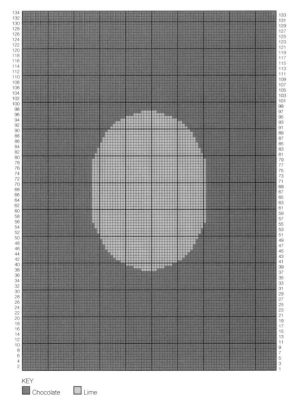

KEY
■ Chocolate □ Lime

front With size 6 (4mm) needles and Chocolate,
cast on 98 sts.
Beg with a k row, work 134 rows in St st from
Chart.
Bind off.

back With size 6 (4mm) needles and Chocolate,
cast on 98 sts.
Beg with a k row, work 134 rows in St st.
Bind off.

to finish Join three sides of Back and Front together,
insert pillow form, and join remaining seam.

gloves

Fingertips of color give a touch of fun to a classic pair of gloves. The cashmere mix yarn makes them soft as well as warm.

size
To fit medium-size woman's hands.

materials
One 50g ball of Debbie Bliss baby cashmerino in Teal (A) and Pale Lilac (B) and small amounts of Dark Lilac (C), Pink (D), Red (E), and Green (F)
Pair each size 2 (3mm) and size 3 (3¼mm) knitting needles

gauge
25 sts and 34 rows to 4in/10cm square over St st using size 3 (3¼mm) needles.

abbreviations
alt = alternate
beg = beginning
cm = centimeters
cont = continue
foll = following
in = inches
inc = increas(e)ing
k = knit
M1 = make one by picking up loop lying between st just worked and next st and working into the back of it
p = purl
rem = remain(ing)
rep = repeat
St st = stockinette stitch
st(s) = stitch(es)
tog = together

right glove

**With size 2 (3mm) needles and A, cast on 44 sts.

Rib row [K1, p1] to end.

Rep the last row 23 times more and inc 6 sts evenly across last row. 50 sts.

Change to size 3 (3¼mm) needles and B.

Beg with a k row, work in St st.

Work 4 rows.**

Thumb shaping

Next row K25, M1, k3, M1, k22.

Work 3 rows.

Next row K25, M1, k5, M1, k22.

P 1 row.

Next row K25, M1, k7, M1, k22.

P 1 row.

Next row K25, M1, k9, M1, k22.

P 1 row.

Cont to inc as set on next and 2 foll alt rows. 64 sts.

P 1 row.

Divide for thumb

Next row K42, turn.

Next row P17, turn and cont on these sts only.

Work 14 rows in St st.

Change to C.

Work 4 rows.

Next row K1, [k2tog] to end.

Break yarn, thread through rem 9 sts, pull tightly to gather and join seam.

With right side facing, rejoin B to base of thumb, k to end. 47 sts.

Work 13 rows.

*****Divide for fingers**

First finger

Next row K30, turn and cast on 2 sts.

Next row P15, turn.

Work 18 rows in St st.

Change to D.

Work 4 rows.

Next row K1, [k2tog] to end.

Break yarn, thread through rem 8 sts, thread tightly to gather, and join seam.

Second finger

With right side facing, rejoin B to base of first finger, pick up and k 2 sts from base of first finger, k6, turn, cast on 2 sts.

Next row P16, turn.

Work 22 rows in St st.

Change to A.

Work 4 rows.

Next row [K2tog] to end.

Break yarn, thread through rem 8 sts, pull tightly to gather, and join seam.

Third finger

With right side facing, join B to base of second finger, pick up and k 2 sts from base of second finger, k6, turn, cast on 2 sts.

Next row P16, turn.

Work 18 rows in St st.

Change to E.

Work 4 rows.

Next row [K2tog] to end.

Break yarn, thread through rem 8 sts, pull tightly to gather, and join seam.

Fourth finger

With right side facing, join B to base of third finger, pick up and k 2 sts from base of third finger, k5, turn.

Next row P12.

Work 12 rows in St st.

Change to F.

Work 4 rows.

Next row [K2tog] to end.

Break yarn, thread through rem 6 sts, pull tightly to gather, and join seam down to cast-on edge.

left glove   Work as given for Right Glove from ** to **.

Thumb shaping

Next row K22, M1, k3, M1, k25.

Work 3 rows.

Next row K22, M1, k5, M1, k25.

P 1 row.

Next row K22, M1, k7, M1, k25.

P 1 row.

Next row K22, M1, k9, M1, k25.

P 1 row.

Cont to inc as set on next and 2 foll alt rows. 64 sts.

P 1 row.

Divide for thumb

Next row K39, turn.

Next row P17, turn and cont on these sts only.

Work 14 rows in St st.

Change to C.

Work 4 rows.

Next row K1, [k2tog] to end.

Break yarn, thread through rem 9 sts, pull tightly to gather, and join seam.

With right side facing, rejoin B to base of thumb, k to end. 47 sts.

Work 13 rows.

Complete as for Right Glove from *** to end.

big spot and diamond cushions

For a strong look, these cushions combine geometric patterning in stripes,

diamonds, and a spot. For a calmer look, you could try using neutral shades.

big spot cushion

size
Approximately 16in/45cm square.

materials
Three 50g balls of Debbie Bliss merino dk in
Red and two 50g balls in Pink
Pair size 6 (4mm) knitting needles
16in/45cm square pillow form

gauge
22 sts and 30 rows to 4in/10cm square over
St st using size 6 (4mm) needles.

abbreviations
beg = beginning
cm = centimeters
in = inches
k = knit
St st = stockinette stitch
st(s) = stitch(es)

note
When working motif, use separate balls of
yarn for each area of color and twist yarns
together on wrong side to avoid holes.

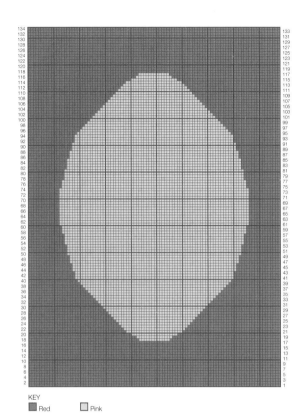

KEY
◼ Red ☐ Pink

front	With size 6 (4mm) needles and Red, cast on 98 sts.
Beg with a k row, work 134 rows in St st from Chart.
Bind off.

back	With size 6 (4mm) needles and Pink, cast on 98 sts.
Beg with a k row, work 134 rows in St st, working in 2-row stripes of Pink and Red.
Bind off in Pink.

to finish	Join three sides of Back and Front together, insert pillow form, and join remaining seam.

diamond cushion

size

Approximately 16in/45cm square.

materials

Two 50g balls of Debbie Bliss merino dk in
each of Red and Pink
Pair size 6 (4mm) knitting needles
16in/45cm square pillow form

gauge

22 sts and 30 rows to 4in/10cm square over
St st using size 6 (4mm) needles.

abbreviations

cm = centimeters

cont = continue

in = inches

k = knit

p = purl

patt = pattern

rep = repeat

St st = stockinette stitch

st(s) = stitch(es)

chart notes

Read right side (k) rows from right to left and
wrong side (p) rows from left to right. When
working motifs, use separate balls of yarn for
each area of color and twist yarns together on
wrong side to avoid holes.

front   With size 6 (4mm) needles and Pink, cast on 98 sts.

Beg with a k row, work in St st from Chart as follows:

1st to 4th rows Work in St st.

5th row K first 9 sts of Chart, work the 16 st patt repeat 5 times, then k the last
9 sts of Chart.

6th row P first 9 sts of Chart, work the 16 st patt repeat 5 times, then p the last
9 sts of Chart.

The 5th and 6th rows set the Chart.

Cont to work all 26 Chart rows.

Rep 1st to 26th rows four times more, then 1st to 4th rows again.

Bind off.

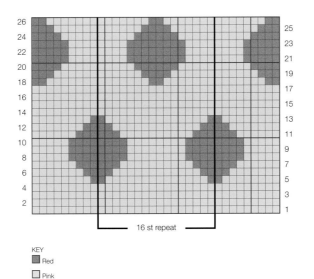

KEY

■ Red

□ Pink

back   With size 6 (4mm) needles and Red, cast on 98 sts.

Beg with a k row, work in St st until 134 rows have been worked.

Bind with Red.

to finish   Join three sides of Back and Front together, insert pillow form, and join

remaining seam.

braided scarf

This unusual scarf is easier to make than it looks. After knitting, the simple ribbed

pieces are braided and secured to make a colorful accessory.

size
Approximately 49in/125cm long.

materials
One 100g ball of Debbie Bliss cashmerino
superchunky in each of Pale Lilac, Lime,
and Plum
Pair size 11 (7½mm) knitting needles

gauge
18 sts and 16 rows to 4in/10cm square over
unstretched rib, using size 11 (7½mm)
needles.

abbreviations
cm = centimeters
in = inches
k = knit
p = purl
st(s) = stitch(es)

strip   Make each of three strips (one in each color) as follows:

With size 11 (7½mm) needles, cast on 11 sts.

1st row (right side) K1, [p1, k1] to end.

2nd row P1, [k1, p1] to end.

These 2 rows form the rib and are repeated.

Work in rib until strip measures approximately 54in/137cm.

Bind off in rib.

to finish   Lay the three strips side by side on a flat surface and stitch the edge of the first 2in/5cm of each strip to the next. Keeping the strips flat, braid them together and stitch the edge of the last 2in/5cm of each strip to the next. Using any loose ends of yarn where possible, catch stitch together the strips where they cross.

socks with cables

Hand-knitted socks in a cashmere mix will add a touch of luxury when you want to take time out and cozy up on a couch or armchair in front of the television or with a good book.

size
One size to fit woman's shoe sizes US 5–7.

materials
Two 50g balls of Debbie Bliss baby cashmerino in Lilac
Set of four size 3 (3¼mm) double-pointed knitting needles

gauge
25 sts and 34 rows to 4in/10cm square over patt using size 3 (3¼mm) needles.

abbreviations
alt = alternate
beg = beginning
C4F = slip next 2 sts onto a cable needle and hold at front of work, k2, then k2 from cable needle
C4B = slip next 2 sts onto a cable needle and hold at back of work, k2, then k2 from cable needle
cm = centimeters
cont = continue
dec = decreas(e)ing
foll = following
in = inches
k = knit
p = purl
patt = pattern
rem = remain(ing)
rep = repeat
skp = slip 1, knit 1, pass slipped stitch over
sl = slip
St st = stockinette stitch
st(s) = stitch(es)
tog = together

to make   With size 3 (3¼mm) double-pointed needles, cast on 54 sts.

(make 2)   Distribute sts evenly, with 18 sts on each of three needles.

Work in rounds as follows:

Rib round *K1, p1; rep from * to end.

Rep the last round 5 times more.

Work in patt as follows:

1st round K11, p1, k4, p1, k21, p1, k4, p1, k10.

2nd round As 1st round.

3rd round K11, p1, C4B, p1, k21, p1, C4F, p1, k10.

4th to 6th rounds As 1st round.

These 6 rounds form the patt and are repeated.

Cont in patt until sock measures 8in/20cm, dec one st over each cable and working 2 sts tog at end of last round. 51 sts.

Cut yarn.

Shape heel

Slip next 13 sts onto first needle, next 13 sts onto second needle, next 13 sts onto 3rd needle, and last 12 sts onto end of first needle.

Rejoin yarn to beg of first needle.

Next row K24, turn.

Next row Sl 1, p22, turn.

Next row Sl 1, k21, turn.

Next row Sl 1, p20, turn.

Cont in this way, working one st less on every row until the foll row has been worked:

Next row Sl 1, p10, turn.

Then work as follows:

Next row Sl 1, k11, turn.

Next row Sl 1, p12, turn.

Cont in this way, working one st more on every row until the foll row has been worked:

Next row Sl 1, p24, turn.

** Slip next 17 sts onto first needle, next 17 sts onto second needle, and next 17 sts onto 3rd needle.

Cont in rounds of st st until sock measures 5½in/14cm from **, dec one st at end of last round. 50 sts.

Shape toe

Next round [K1, skp, k19, k2tog, k1] twice.

Next round K to end.

Next round [K1, skp, k17, k2tog, k1] twice.

Next round K to end.

Next round [K1, skp, k15, k2tog, k1] twice.

Next round K to end.

Cont in rounds, dec on every alt round as set until the foll round has been worked:

Next round [K1, skp, k7, k2tog, k1] twice. 22 sts.

Slip first 11 sts onto one needle and rem 11 sts onto a second needle.

Fold sock inside out and bind off, taking one st from each needle together.

spot blanket

Vibrant spots in clashing colors create an area of vibrancy against the cool

minimalism of this contemporary bedroom.

size
Approximately 45½ x 72in/116 x 183cm.

materials
Nineteen 50g balls of Debbie Bliss merino
aran in Red and eighteen balls in Pink
Pair size 8 (5mm) knitting needles
Size G-6 (4mm) crochet hook

gauge
18 sts and 24 rows to 4in/10cm square over
st st using size 8 (5mm) needles.

abbreviations
ch = chain
cm = centimeters
sc = single crochet
in = inches
k = knit
p = purl
rep = repeat
St st = stockinette stitch
st(s) = stitch(es)

chart notes
Read right side (k) rows from right to left and
wrong side (p) rows from left to right. When
working motif, use separate balls of yarn for
each area of color and twist yarns together on
wrong side to avoid holes.

first panel	With size 8 (5mm) needles and Red, cast on 32 sts.
	Beg with a k row, work in St st from Chart.
	Work 1st to 40th rows from Chart, working circle motif in Pink.
	Change to Pink.
	Beg with a k row, work in St st from Chart.
	Work 1st to 40th rows from Chart, working circle motif in Red.
	Rep the last 80 rows four times more and 1st to 40th rows again.
	Bind off in Red.
second panel	With size 8 (5mm) needles and Pink cast on 32 sts.
	Beg with a k row, work in St st from Chart.
	Work 1st to 40th rows from Chart, working circle motif in Red.
	Change to Red.
	Work 1st to 40th rows from Chart, working circle motif in Pink.
	Rep the last 80 rows four times more and 1st to 40th rows again.
	Bind off in Pink.
third, fifth, and seventh panels	Work as First Panel.
fourth and sixth panels	Work as Second Panel.

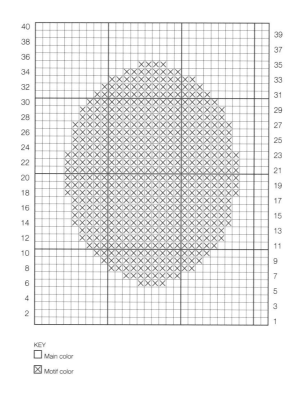

KEY
☐ Main color
☒ Motif color

to finish   Join the panels together so that the edge of the Second Panel is joined to the edge of the First, the edge of the Third is joined to the Second, and so on.
Edging: With right side facing and size G-6 (4mm) crochet hook, join Red to any corner and work as follows: ch2 to count as first sc, work sc all around outer edge of blanket, join with a slip st to 2nd of 2ch. Fasten off.

felted bag

This bag is knitted in an alpaca silk yarn, so that even after felting it retains a beautiful softness.

size
Approximately 12¼ x 12¼in/31 x 31cm.

materials
Seven 50g balls of Debbie Bliss alpaca silk in Lime
Size 8 (5mm) circular needle

gauge
18 sts and 24 rows to 4in/10cm square over St st before felting, using size 8 (5mm) needles.

abbreviations
beg = beginning
cm = centimeters
cont = continue
in = inches
inc = increas(e)ing
k = knit
kfb = k into front and back of st
p = purl
St st = stockinette stitch
st(s) = stitch(es)

note
You may find it easier to work the base using a pair of size 8 (5mm) needles and then change to the circular needle to work the main bag.

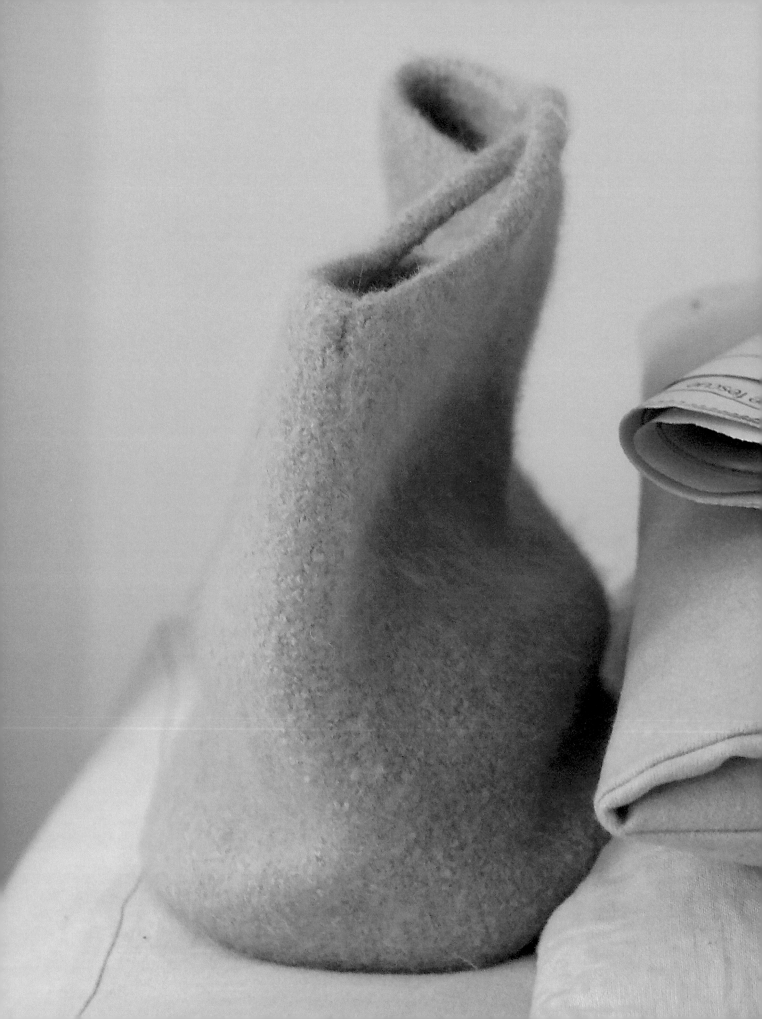

base   With size 8 (5mm) circular needle, cast on 5 sts.

1st row (right side) [Kfb] 4 times, k1. 9 sts.

2nd and all wrong side rows Purl.

3rd row [Kfb] 8 times, k1. 17 sts.

5th row [K1, kfb] 8 times, k1. 25 sts.

7th row [K2, kfb] 8 times, k1. 33 sts.

9th row [K3, kfb] 8 times, k1. 41 sts.

Cont to work in St st and inc 8 sts across every right side row as set, working one st more before each inc as before until there are 137 sts, ending with a right side row.

main bag   **1st ridge row** (wrong side) Knit.

2nd ridge row (right side) Purl.

Beg with a p row, work in St st until bag measures 17in/43cm from 2nd ridge row, ending with a k row.

Next row (wrong side) Knit.

Next row Purl.

Next row K21, bind off 26, k next 41 sts, bind off 26, k to end.

Next row (right side) Purl and cast on 26 sts over each set of 26 sts bound off in previous row.

Next row Knit.

Next row Purl.

Next row Bind off knitwise.

to finish   Join seam from top edge to ridge row, then across the base. Darn in all yarn ends.

to felt the bag   Place the knitted bag in the washing machine with other objects (I use old sneakers tied inside a pillowcase) and wash on the highest heat setting with the maximum spin speed. Remove from the machine, gently pull into shape, and leave to dry.

modern country

cable and seed stitch bag

A chunky cable decorates this multicolored bag, which is lined with gingham fabric to give it extra durability. It makes a great little bag for carrying your knitting around.

size

Approximately 8¾in/22cm wide x 6in/15cm high excluding handles.

materials

Two 100g hanks of Debbie Bliss maya or four 50g balls of Debbie Bliss SoHo in shade 09
Pair each size 11 (8mm) and size 9 (5½mm) knitting needles
½yd/0.5m lining fabric
Sewing thread
24in/60cm polythene tubing

gauge

12 sts and 16 rows to 4in/10cm square over St st using size 11 (8mm) needles and two strands of yarn held together.

abbreviations

C8B = slip next 4 sts onto cable needle and hold at back of work, k4, then k4 from cable needle

C8F = slip next 4 sts onto cable needle and hold at front of work, k4, then k4 from cable needle

cm = centimeters

in = inches

k = knit

kfb = knit into front and back of next st to make one st

kfpb = knit into front and purl into back of next st to make one st

p = purl

pfkb = purl into front and knit into back of next st to make one st

rep = repeat

st(s) = stitch(es)

tog = together

to make With size 11 (8mm) needles and two strands of yarn, cast on 29 sts.

1st row K1, [p1, k1] to end.

2nd row As 1st row.

3rd row (right side) K1, p1, k1, k7, [kfb] 4 times, p1, [kfb] 4 times, k7, k1, p1, k1. 37 sts.

4th row K1, p1, k1, p15, k1, p15, k1, p1, k1.

5th row Pfkb, p1, k1, k7, C8B, p1, C8F, k7, k1, pfkb, p1. 39 sts.

6th row [P1, k1] twice, p15, k1, p15, [k1, p1] twice.

7th row [P1, k1] twice, k15, p1, k15, [k1, p1] twice.

8th to 12th rows Rep 6th and 7th rows twice more and 6th row again.

13th row Kfpb, k1, p1, k1, k7, C8B, p1, C8F, k7, k1, p1, kfpb, k1. 41 sts.

14th row K1, [p1, k1] twice, p15, k1, p15, k1, [p1, k1] twice.

15th row K1, [p1, k1] twice, k15, p1, k15, k1, [p1, k1] twice.

16th to 20th rows Rep 14th and 15th rows twice more and 14th row again.

21st row Pfkb, [p1, k1] twice, k7, C8B, p1, C8F, k7, k1, p1, k1, pfkb, p1. 43 sts.

22nd row [P1, k1] 3 times, p15, k1, p15, [k1, p1] 3 times.

23rd row [P1, k1] 3 times, k15, p1, k15, [k1, p1] 3 times.

24th to 28th rows Rep 22nd and 23rd rows twice more and 22nd row again.

29th row Kfpb, k1, [p1, k1] twice, k7, C8B, p1, C8F, k7, [k1, p1] twice, kfpb, k1. 45 sts.

30th row K1, [p1, k1] 3 times, p15, k1, p15, k1, [p1, k1] 3 times.

Shape for base

31st row (right side) Bind off 7 sts, k next 14 sts, p1, k15, k1, [p1, k1] 3 times.

32nd row Bind off 7 sts, p next 14 sts, k1, p15. 31 sts.

33rd row K15, p1, k15.

34th row P15, k1, p15.

Rep the last 2 rows 4 times more.

43rd row (right side) Cast on 7 sts and work k1, [p1, k1] 3 times across these sts, k15, p1, k15.

44th row Cast on 7 sts, work k1, [p1, k1] 3 times across these sts, p15, k1, p15, k1, [p1, k1] 3 times. 45 sts.

45th row (right side) K1, [p1, k1] 3 times, k15, p1, k15, k1, [p1, k1] 3 times.

46th row K1, [p1, k1] 3 times, p15, k1, p15, k1, [p1, k1] 3 times.

47th row P2tog, k1, [p1, k1] twice, k7, C8B, p1, C8F, k7, [k1, p1] twice, k1, p2tog. 43 sts.

48th row [P1, k1] 3 times, p15, k1, p15, [k1, p1] 3 times.

49th row [P1, k1] 3 times, k15, p1, k15, [k1, p1] 3 times.

50th to 54th rows Rep 48th and 49th rows twice more and 48th row again.

55th row K2tog, [p1, k1] twice, k7, C8B, p1, C8F, k7, [k1, p1] twice, k2tog. 41 sts.

56th row K1, [p1, k1] twice, p15, k1, p15, k1, [p1, k1] twice.

57th row K1, [p1, k1] twice, k15, p1, k15, k1, [p1, k1] twice.

58th to 62nd rows Rep 56th and 57th rows twice more and 56th row again.

63rd row P2tog, k1, p1, k1, k7, C8B, p1, C8F, k7, k1, p1, k1, p2tog. 39 sts.

64th row [P1, k1] twice, p15, k1, p15, [k1, p1] twice.

65th row [P1, k1] twice, k15, p1, k15, [k1, p1] twice.

66th to 70th rows Rep 64th and 65th rows twice more and 64th row again.

71st row K2tog, p1, k1, k7, C8B, p1, C8F, k7, k1, p1, k2tog. 37 sts.

72nd row K1, p1, k1, p15, k1, p15, k1, p1, k1.

73rd row K1, p1, k1, k7, [k2tog] 4 times, p1, [k2tog] 4 times, k7, k1, p1, k1. 29 sts.

74th row K1, [p1, k1] to end.

75th row As 74th row.

Bind off in seed st.

handles
(make 2)

With size 9 (5½mm) needles and one strand of yarn, cast on 7 sts.

Seed st row K1, [p1, k1] 3 times.

Rep the last row until strip measures 13½in/34cm.

Bind off in seed st.

to finish

Lay the bag flat on the lining fabric and use as a template to cut the lining, allowing an extra 1.5cm/⅝in of fabric all around. Sew the side seams on the knitted bag from the cast-on/bound-off edges down to the base shaping. Sew bound-off/cast-on edges of base shaping to row ends of base. Prepare lining in the same way. Sew 1¼in/3cm of each end of the handle strips to the inside of the front and the back of the bag. Cut the plastic tubing into two 12in/30cm lengths and make a ¾in/2cm diagonal cut across each end of the two pieces. Make two holes in each end of the tubing pieces and use these to stitch the tubing to the inside of the bag where the handles have been attached. Fold the handles around the tubing and stitch the seam. Insert the lining into the bag and slip stitch around the top edge, so hiding the ends of the handles.

cabled slippers

Knitted slippers are great for relaxing in around the house. Knitted in cotton with cables, they are a sturdier alternative to socks.

sizes
To fit woman's shoe sizes   5–6   7–8

materials
2(3) 50g balls of Debbie Bliss cotton dk in Terracotta
Pair size 6 (4mm) knitting needles
Pair of insoles the appropriate size
Lining fabric and fabric glue

gauge
20 sts and 28 rows to 4in/10cm square over St st using size 6 (4mm) needles.

abbreviations
C4B = slip next 2 sts onto a cable needle and hold at back of work, k2, then k2 from cable needle
C4F = slip next 2 sts onto a cable needle and hold at front of work, k2, then k2 from cable needle
Tw2L = k into back of 2nd st on left needle, k into front of first st, then slip both sts off left needle together

Tw2R = k into front of 2nd st on left needle, k into front of first st, then slip both sts off needle together
beg = beginning
cm = centimeters
cont = continue
dec = decreas(e)ing
foll = following
in = inches
inc = increas(e)ing
k = knit
p = purl
patt = pattern
rem = remain(ing)
st(s) = stitch(es)
tog = together

note
The slippers are worked in one piece, starting with the upper and working toward the toe, then working the sole, ending at the heel. Sizings are approximate, as knitted fabric is elastic.

left slipper

Upper

With size 6 (4mm) needles, cast on 68(74) sts.

1st row (right side) P8(11), [Tw2R, p3] 3 times, [k4, p5] twice, k4, [p3, Tw2R] 3 times, p8(11).

2nd row K8(11), [p2, k3] 3 times, [p4, k5] twice, p4, [k3, p2] 3 times, k8(11).

3rd row Bind off 3 sts, p next 4(7) sts, [Tw2R, p3] 3 times, [C4B, p5] twice, C4B, [p3, Tw2R] 3 times, p8(11).

4th row Bind off 3 sts, k next 4(7) sts, [p2, k3] 3 times, [p4, k5] twice, p4, [k3, p2] 3 times, k5(8). 62(68) sts.

These 4 rows set the position of the twist sts and cables.

Cont in patt and bind off 4 sts at beg of next 4 rows and then 3 sts at beg of foll 0(2) rows. 46 sts.

Next row P2tog, patt to last 2 sts, p2tog. 44 sts.

Patt 5(3) rows.

Next row K2tog, k1, p3, Tw2R, p3, C4B, p3, p2tog, C4B, p2tog, p3, C4B, p3, Tw2R, p3, k1, k2tog. 40 sts.

Next row [P2, k3] twice, p4, [k4, p4] twice, [k3, p2] twice.

Patt 4 rows as now set, working cables on 3rd of these 4 rows.

Next row K2tog, p3, Tw2R, p3, k4, p2, p2tog, k4, p2tog, p2, k4, p3, Tw2R, p3, k2tog. 36 sts.

Cont in patt and dec one st at each end of 4th(6th) and foll 4th(6th) row and then of every foll 4th row until 24 sts rem.

Patt 1(3) rows.

Bind off 2 sts at beg of next 6 rows and 3 sts at beg of foll row. 9 sts.

Next row (wrong side) Bind off 3 sts, p1, p2tog, p1, k1. 5 sts.

Sole

Seed st row K1, [p1, k1] twice.

(Rep last row once more for Right Slipper only.)

Next row Inc in first st, seed st to last st, inc in last st. 7 sts.

Seed st 1 row.

Rep the last 2 rows 5(6) times more. 17(19) sts.

Work 20(22) rows in seed st.

Next row Work 2tog, seed st to end.

Seed st 3 rows.

Rep the last 4 rows 2(3) times more. 14(15) sts.

Seed st 28(30) rows.

Bind off 2 sts at beg of next 4(6) rows. 6(3) sts.

Bind off.

right slipper Work exactly as for Left Slipper, working C4F for C4B and Tw2L for Tw2R and noting instruction for Right Slipper in parentheses.

to finish Making sure that slippers are mirror images, join ends of cast-on edge and row ends of 1st row together to form center back seam. Slip stitch sole to upper around edge. Using the insoles as templates, cut out two pieces of fabric allowing an extra ½in/1cm all around the edge. Cover the insoles with fabric, turn the excess onto the underside, and glue in place. Slip the insoles into the slippers, and catch in place with a few stitches.

felted cozies

Create a contemporary classic with a modern take on the teapot cozy. Felted after

knitting, it is both practical and stylish. Make egg cozies to match.

sizes

Teapot cozy to fit a medium-sized teapot.
Egg cozy (not shown) to fit a medium-sized
egg in an eggcup

materials

Teapot cozy—Four 50g balls of Debbie Bliss
alpaca silk in Coral
Egg cozy—One 50g ball per two cozies
Pair size 8 (5mm) knitting needles
Contrasting yarn for pompon

gauge

18 sts and 24 rows to 4in/10cm square over
St st, before felting, using size 8 (5mm)
needles.

abbreviations

alt = alternate

cm = centimeters

dec = decreas(e)ing

foll = following

in = inches

k = knit

rem = remain(ing)

St st = stockinette stitch

st(s) = stitch(es)

tbl = through back of loop

tog = together

note

Before washing/felting, the cozy will appear to
be far too big, but the fabric will shrink.

to make **teapot** **cozy** (make 2 halves)	With size 8 (5mm) needles, cast on 67 sts. K 1 row. Beg with a k row, work 30 rows in St st. **Shape top** **Next row** (right side) K2tog tbl, k to last 2 sts, k2tog. Cont in St st and dec one st as set at each end of 7 foll 4th rows, then 2 foll alt rows. P 1 row. Bind off 2 sts at beg of next 8 rows, then 4 sts at beg of foll 6 rows. Bind off rem 7 sts.
to make **egg cozy** (not shown) (make 2 halves)	With size 8 (5mm) needles, cast on 22 sts. K 1 row. Beg with a k row, work 12 rows in St st. **Shape top** **Next row** (right side) K2tog tbl, k to last 2 sts, k2tog. Cont in St st and dec one st as set at each end of 4 foll 4th rows. 12 sts. P 1 row. Bind off 2 sts at beg of next 4 rows. Bind off rem 4 sts.
to felt the **fabric**	Darn in all yarn ends. Place knitted pieces in the washing machine with other objects (I use old sneakers tied inside a pillowcase) and wash on the highest heat setting with the maximum spin speed. Remove from the machine, gently unroll the felted fabric pieces around the edges, pull into shape, and leave to dry flat.
to finish	Place the two felted pieces together and stitch around the shaped edge, leaving the cast-on edges open. Make a pompon from contrasting yarn (see opposite) and sew to top of cozy.

pompon

1   Cut two circles from cardboard that are slightly smaller than the diameter of the pompon required. Make a central hole through both circles approximately one-third of the diameter. Place both rings together, one on top of the other, lining up the holes.

2   Thread yarn onto a darning needle and wrap the yarn through the hole and around the outer edge, ensuring that all the cardboard is covered. Continue until the hole in the center is completely filled and it is impossible to force the needle through the center. This will ensure that the pompon is as firm and neat as possible.

3   Ease the two circles of cardboard apart and cut all the strands between the circles. Do not remove the cardboard until a tightly tied double strand of yarn has been secured around the center of all the strands, leaving a length free to sew the pompon in place. Remove the cardboard and trim any straggly ends of yarn.

seed stitch jacket

Here is a cozy jacket made in a beautiful alpaca and silk yarn to create a luxurious but relaxed jacket for a country weekend.

sizes

To fit bust	32–34	36–38	40–42	in
	82–87	92–97	102–107	cm

finished knitted measurements

Bust	45¼	51¼	57	in
	115	130	145	cm
Length to shoulder	26	26½	26¾	in
	66	67	68	cm
Sleeve length	17	17¼	17¾	in
	43	44	45	cm

materials

24(26:28) 50g balls of Debbie Bliss alpaca silk in Coral
Pair size 8 (5mm) knitting needles
Long size 8 (5mm) circular needle
5 buttons

gauge

16 sts and 28 rows to 4in/10cm square over patt using size 8 (5mm) needles.

abbreviations

yo twice = yarn around needle twice to make 2 sts
alt = alternate
beg = beginning
cm = centimeters
cont = continue
foll = following
in = inches
k = knit
p = purl
patt = pattern
rem = remain(ing)
rep = repeat
St st = stockinette stitch
st(s) = stitch(es)
tog = together

back With size 8 (5mm) needles, cast on 94(106:118) sts.

1st row (right side) K2, [p2, k2] to end.

2nd row P2, [k2, p2] to end.

Rep the last 2 rows once more.

Now work in patt as follows:

1st row P2, [k2, p2] to end.

2nd row K2, [p2, k2] to end.

3rd row K2, [p2, k2] to end.

4th row P2, [k2, p2] to end.

These 4 rows form the patt and are repeated throughout.

Cont in patt until back measures 26(26½:26¾)in/66(67:68)cm from beg, ending with a wrong side row.

Shape shoulders

Bind off 16(19:21) sts at beg of next 2 rows and 17(19:22) sts at beg of foll 2 rows.

Bind off rem 28(30:32) sts.

pocket With size 8 (5mm) needles, cast on 27 sts.

linings Beg with a k row, work 7in/18cm in st st, ending with a p row and decreasing 3 sts evenly across last row. 24 sts. Leave sts on a holder.

left front With size 8 (5mm) needles, cast on 43(51:59) sts.

1st row (right side) K2, [p2, k2] to last 5 sts, p2, k3.

2nd row P3, [k2, p2] to end.

Rep the last 2 rows once more.

Work in patt as follows:

1st row P2, [k2, p2] to last 5 sts, k2, p3.

2nd row K3, [p2, k2] to end.

3rd row K2, [p2, k2] to last 5 sts, p2, k3.

4th row P3, [k2, p2] to end.

These 4 rows form the patt and are repeated throughout.

Cont in patt until front measures 8in/20cm from cast-on edge, ending with a wrong side row.

Pocket opening

Next row Patt 12(16:20), bind off next 24 sts in patt, patt to end.

Next row Patt 7(11:15), work in patt across 24 sts of pocket lining, patt to end.

Cont in patt until front measures same as Back to shoulder shaping, ending at side edge.

Shape shoulders
Bind off 16(19:21) sts at beg of next row and 17(19:22) sts at beg of foll alt row.
Leave rem 10(13:16) sts on a holder.

right front   With size 8 (5mm) needles, cast on 43(51:59) sts.
1st row (right side) K3, [p2, k2] to end.
2nd row P2, [k2, p2] to last 5 sts, k2, p3.
Rep the last 2 rows once more.
Work in patt as follows:
1st row P3, [k2, p2] to end.
2nd row K2, [p2, k2] to last 5 sts, p2, k3.
3rd row K3, [p2, k2] to end.
4th row P2, [k2, p2] to last 5 sts, k2, p3.
These 4 rows form the patt and are repeated throughout.
Cont in patt until front measures 8in/20cm from cast-on edge, ending with a wrong side row.
Pocket opening
Next row Patt 7(11:15), bind off next 24 sts in patt, patt to end.
Next row Patt 12(16:20), work in patt across 24 sts of pocket lining, patt to end.
Cont in patt until front measures same as Back to shoulder shaping, ending at side edge.
Shape shoulders
Bind off 16(19:21) sts at beg of next row and 17(19:22) sts at beg of foll alt row.
Leave rem 10(13:16) sts on a holder.

sleeves   With size 8 (5mm) needles, cast on 46(50:54) sts.
Work 4 rows rib as given for Back.
Cont in patt as given for Back and inc one st at each end of the 5th and every foll 8th row until there are 72(76:80) sts.
Work even until sleeve measures 17(17¼:17¾)in/43(44:45)cm from cast-on edge, ending with a wrong side row.
Bind off.

collar   Join shoulder seams.
With right side facing and size 8 (5mm) needles, slip 10(13:16) sts from right front onto a needle, cast on 48(50:52) sts for center back neck, then patt across 10(13:16) sts from left front. 68(76:84) sts.
Work 6in/15cm in patt across all sts, as set by sts from front holders.
Bind off.

button band   On the left front, mark a point 14in/35cm down from bound-off edge of collar. With wrong side of jacket facing and size 8 (5mm) needles, pick up and k 75 sts from marker to bound-off edge of collar. Break off yarn and slip these sts onto the size 8 (5mm) circular needle.

With right side of jacket facing and using the same size 8 (5mm) circular needle, pick up and k 91(91:95) sts from marker to cast-on edge. 166(166:170) sts.

Work backward and forward in rib as follows:

1st row (wrong side) P2, [k2, p2] to end.

2nd row K2, [p2, k2] to end.

Rep the last 2 rows 8 times more.

Bind off in rib.

buttonhole band   On the right front, mark a point 14in/35cm down from bound-off edge of collar. With wrong side of jacket facing and size 8 (5mm) needles, pick up and k 75 sts from bound-off edge of collar to marker. Break off yarn and leave sts on needle.

With right side of jacket facing and size 8 (5mm) circular needle, pick up and k 91(91:95) sts from cast-on edge to marker. Break off yarn, slip sts from needle onto the circular needle. 166(166:170) sts.

Rejoin yarn to other end of circular needle at the cast-on edge.

Work backward and forward in rib as follows:

1st row (right side) K2, [p2, k2] to end.

2nd row P2, [k2, p2] to end.

Rep the last 2 rows 3 times more.

Buttonhole row (right side) Rib 4, [k2tog, yo twice, p2tog tbl, rib 14, p2tog, yo twice, skpo, rib 14] once more, k2tog, y2rn, p2tog tbl, rib to end.

Work 9 rows more in rib.

Bind off in rib.

to finish   With center of bound-off edge of sleeve at shoulder, sew on sleeves. Sew cast-on edge of collar to bound-off sts of center back neck, easing in fullness. Slip stitch pocket linings in place. Join side and sleeve seams. Sew on buttons.

seed stitch wrap

Relax into the perfect snuggly throw that is worked in a soft alpaca blend to create

real coziness and warmth. Every home needs one.

size
17¾ x 67in/45 x 170cm.

abbreviations
cm = centimeters
in = inches
k = knit
p = purl
rep = repeat
st(s) = stitch(es)

materials
Twelve 50g balls of Debbie Bliss alpaca silk
in Plum
Pair size 9 (5½mm) knitting needles

gauge
15 sts and 31 rows to 4in/10cm square over
seed st using size 9 (5½mm) needles.

to make With size 9 (5½mm) needles, cast on 67 sts.
Seed st row K1, [p1, k1] to end.
Rep this row until throw measures 67in/170cm.
Bind off in seed st.

pot holder

Here is a wonderfully easy knit to make. Worked in seed stitch and lined with a contrasting fabric, it is practical and adds a homey touch to your kitchen.

size
7 x 7in/18 x 18cm

materials
One 50g ball of Debbie Bliss cotton dk in Taupe
Pair size 8 (5mm) knitting needles
7¾ x 7¾in/20 x 20cm piece of fabric
5in/13cm tape or ribbon

gauge
17 sts and 24 rows to 4in/10cm square over seed st using size 8 (5mm) needles and two strands of yarn held together.

abbreviations
cm = centimeters
in = inches
k = knit
p = purl
st(s) = stitch(es)

to make   Wind off 25g of yarn into a separate ball, so making two equal balls of yarn.
With size 8 (5mm) needles and two strands of yarn held together, cast on 27 sts.
Seed st row K1, [p1, k1] to end.
Rep this row 41 times more.
Bind off in seed st.

lining   Fold tape/ribbon in half to form a loop and stitch to the wrong side of one corner of the knitted piece. Press ⅝in/1½cm onto the wrong side of the fabric on all edges, mitering the corners. Slip stitch the fabric in place to the wrong side of the knitted piece, ¼in/5mm in from the edges, covering the ends of the tape/ribbon.

ribbed scarf

This quick and easy scarf is knitted in a space-dyed yarn that creates rustic tonal effects without having to use more than one yarn.

size
Approximately 4¾ x 59in/12 x 150cm, without stretching.

materials
Two 100g hanks of Debbie Bliss maya or four 50g balls of Debbie Bliss SoHo shade 06
Pair size 9 (5½mm) knitting needles

gauge
25 sts and 24 rows to 4in/10cm square over unstretched patt using size 9 (5½mm) needles.

abbreviations
cm = centimeters
in = inches
k = knit
p = purl
patt = pattern
st(s) = stitch(es)

to make
With size 9 (5½mm) needles, cast on 31 sts.
1st row [K2, p2] to last 3 sts, k2, p1.
This row forms the patt and is repeated throughout.
Work in patt until scarf measures approximately 59in/150cm from cast-on edge, or until you have used almost two whole hanks or four balls.
Bind off in patt.

washcloth

This has to be the simplest of items to make. Worked throughout in knit stitches, it is

a perfect first project for a beginner.

size
7 x 6in/18 x 15cm.

materials
One 50g ball of Debbie Bliss cotton dk in
Cream
Pair size 10½ (6½mm) knitting needles

gauge
14 sts and 25 rows to 4in/10cm square over
garter st using size 10½ (6½mm) needles and
two strands of yarn used together.

abbreviations

cm = centimeters

in = inches

k = knit

st(s) = stitch(es)

to make   Wind off 25g of yarn into a separate ball, so making two equal balls of yarn.
With size 10½ (6½mm) needles and two strands of yarn held together, cast
on 25 sts.
Work 36 rows in garter st (k every row).
Bind off.
Make a small hanging loop on one corner of the washcloth.

woven cushion

This simple cushion is decorated by weaving in a contrasting yarn. The yarn used

here is space-dyed, which creates a subtle shaded effect.

size
Approximately 16in/40cm square.

materials
Five 50g balls of Debbie Bliss cashmerino
aran in Stone (A)
One 100g hank of Debbie Bliss maya (B) in
shade 06 or two 50g balls of Debbie Bliss
SoHo (B)
Pair size 8 (5mm) knitting needles
16in/40cm square pillow form

gauge
18 sts and 24 rows to 4in/10cm square over
St st using size 8 (5mm) needles.

abbreviations
cm = centimeters
in = inches
k = knit
p = purl
patt = pattern
rep = repeat
St st = stockinette stitch
st(s) = stitch(es)

to make
With size 8 (5mm) needles and A, cast on 73 sts.

K 3 rows.

Beg with a k row, work 9¾in/25cm in St st, ending with a k row.

Ridge row (wrong side) Knit.

Now work in patt as follows:

1st row (right side) [K3, p1, k2] to last st, k1.

2nd row Purl.

3rd row K1, [p1, k1] to end.

4th row Purl.

5th and 6th rows As 3rd and 4th rows.

7th to 10th rows Rep 1st and 2nd rows twice more.

Repeat these 10 rows 9 times more, then work 1st to 5th rows once more.

Ridge row (wrong side) Knit.

Beg with a k row, work in St st for a further 9½in/24cm, ending with a k row.

K 2 rows.

Bind off knitwise.

to finish
Fold the cushion cover in three along the two ridge rows with the cast-on and bound-off edges overlapping to form the opening for the cushion back. Join the side seams. Insert the pillow form first, then weave two strands of contrasting yarn B vertically and horizontally through the cover, using the grid pattern as a guide. By working with the pillow form inside the cover, you will not pull the woven yarn too tight or leave it too loose.

seaside

diagonal-front jacket

This casual jacket's unusual structure is created by simply increasing and decreasing to form diagonal ribbed fronts.

sizes

To fit bust	32–36	38–42	in
	81–92	97–107	cm

finished knitted measurements

Bust	39½	45½	in
	100	116	cm
Length	21¼	24¾	in
	54	63	cm
Sleeve seam (with cuff turned back)			
	17¼	19	in
	44	48	cm

materials

16(18) 50g balls of Debbie Bliss cotton dk in Pale Blue

Pair size 6 (4mm) knitting needles

Long size 6 (4mm) circular needle

gauge

19 sts and 28 rows to 4in/10cm square over patt using size 6 (4mm) needles.

abbreviations

cm = centimeters

cont = continue

dec = decreas(e)ing

foll = following

in = inches

inc = increas(e)ing

k = knit

kfb = k into front and back of st

M1 = make one by picking up loop lying between st just worked and next st and working into the back of it

p = purl

patt = pattern

rem = remain(ing)

sl = slip

st(s) = stitch(es)

tbl = through back of loop

tog = together

basic stitch pattern

back and fronts

1st row (right side) K3, [p1, k3] to end.

2nd row Purl.

These 2 rows form the basic stitch pattern.

(The back and fronts are worked in one piece to armholes as follows:)

With size 6 (4mm) circular needle, cast on 215(247) sts.

1st row (right side) K59(67), kfb, [k3, p1] 23(27) times, k2, kfb, k2tog tbl, turn.

Next row Sl 1, p97(113), p2tog, turn.

Next row Sl 1, p1, M1, [k3, p1] 23(27) times, k3, M1, p1, k1, k2tog tbl, turn.

Next row Sl 1, p101(117), p2tog, turn.

Next row Sl 1, k1, p1, k1, M1, [k3, p1] 23(27) times, k3, M1, k1, p1, k2, k2tog tbl, turn.

Next row Sl 1, p105(121), p2tog, turn.

Next row Sl 1, k2, p1, k2, M1, [k3, p1] 23(27) times, k3, M1, k2, p1, k3, k2tog tbl, turn.

Next row Sl 1, p109(125), p2tog, turn.

Next row Sl 1, k3, p1, k3, M1, [k3, p1] 23(27) times, k3, M1, k3, p1, k3, p1, k2tog tbl, turn.

Next row Sl 1, p113(129), p2tog, turn.

Next row Sl 1, p1, [k3, p1] twice, M1, [k3, p1] 23(27) times, k3, M1, [p1, k3] twice, p1, k1, k2tog tbl, turn.

Next row Sl 1, p117(133), p2tog, turn.

Next row Sl 1, k1, p1, [k3, p1] twice, k1, M1, [k3, p1] 23(27) times, k3, M1, k1, [p1, k3] twice, p1, k2, k2tog tbl, turn.

Next row Sl 1, p121(137), p2tog, turn.

These turning rows set the way in which cast-on sts are taken into work at each side for the Fronts. Cont to inc one st at each side of center 95(111) sts on every right side row and work 2 more sts tog at end of every row, slipping the previous row's worked tog st at beg of every row. Cont in this way until all cast-on sts have been worked and taken into the basic stitch patt, so ending with a wrong side row.

Cont to inc one st at each side of center 95(111) sts on next and every foll right side row taking inc sts into patt and working p1 at each end of every right side row, until there are 223(255) sts, ending with a wrong side p row.

Next row (right side) P2tog, patt 62(70), M1, patt 95(111), M1, patt 62(70), p2tog.

Next row Purl.

Keeping patt correct, rep the last 2 rows 11(19) times more, ending with a p row.

right front

Divide for Back and Fronts

Next row (right side) With size 6 (4mm) needles, p2tog, patt 62(70), turn and cont on these sts only, leave rem sts on the circular needle.

Next row (wrong side) P63(71).

Next row P2tog, patt 61(69).

Next row P62(70).

Next row P2tog, patt 60(68).

Cont in this way to dec one st at beg of every right side row until 32(36) sts rem, ending with a p row.

Do not cut yarn, leave sts on a holder.

back

With right side facing, size 6 (4mm) needles, and a new ball of yarn, work across rem sts on circular needle as follows: k3, p2tog, patt 85(101), p2tog, k3, turn and cont on these 93(109) sts only, leave rem sts on the circular needle.

Next row (wrong side) P93(109).

Next row K3, p2tog, patt 83(99), p2tog, k3.

Next row P91(107).

Next row K3, p2tog, patt 81(97), p2tog, k3.

Cont in this way to dec one st at each end of every right side row until 31(39) sts rem, ending with a p row.

Cut yarn and leave sts on a holder.

left front

With right side facing and size 6 (4mm) needles, rejoin yarn to rem sts on circular needle, patt to last 2 sts, p2tog.

Next row (wrong side) Purl.

Next row Patt to last 2 sts, p2tog.

Cont in this way to dec one st at end of every foll right side row until 32(36) sts rem, ending with a p row.

Leave sts on a holder.

sleeves

Cuff

With size 6 (4mm) needles, cast on 43(47) sts.

1st row (right side) K1, [p1, k3] to last 2 sts, p1, k1.

2nd row Purl.

These 2 rows set the patt.

Work in patt until sleeve measures 3¼in/8cm, ending with a right side row.

Ridge row (wrong side) Knit.

Next row (right side) Knit.

Now reverse the patt for the main sleeve as follows:

Next row (right side) K1, [p1, k3] to last 2 sts, p1, k1.

Next row Purl.

Cont in patt as set for a further 3¼in/8cm, ending with a p row.

Next row (right side) K1, M1, patt to last st, M1, k1.

Cont in patt and inc one st in the same way, at each end of every foll 4th row until there are 75(71) sts, then at each end of every foll 6th row until there are 83(87) sts.

Work even until sleeve measures 17¼(19)in/44(48)cm from ridge row, ending with a p row.

Shape raglans

Next row (right side) K1, p2tog, patt to last 3 sts, p2tog, k1.

Next row Purl.

Rep these 2 rows until 19(15) sts rem, ending with a p row.

Leave sts on a holder.

collar
With right side facing and size 6 (4mm) circular needle, work across sts on holders as follows: work p2tog, patt 29(33) across right front, k last st tog with first st of right sleeve, [p1, k3] 4(3) times, p1, k last st tog with first st of back, k2, [p1, k3] 6(8) times, p1, k2, k last st tog with first st of left sleeve, [p1, k3] 4(3) times, p1, k last st tog with first st of left front, k2, patt to last 2 sts, p2tog. 125(137) sts.

Next row (wrong side) Purl.

Next row (right side) P2tog, patt to last 2 sts, p2tog.

Rep these 2 rows until collar measures 3¼in/8cm, ending with a right side row. Bind off knitwise.

to finish
Join raglan seams, matching row for row. Join sleeve seams.

child's denim sweater

This very easy child's sweater in my denim yarn knits up quickly and simply and so is ideal for the novice knitter.

sizes

To fit ages	2	3	4	years
finished knitted measurements				
Chest	28	31½	34¾	in
	71	80	88	cm
Length	13¾	15	16½	in
	35	38	42	cm
Sleeve seam	8¾	9¾	11	in
	22	25	28	cm

materials

6(7:8) 50g balls of Debbie Bliss cotton denim aran in Medium Blue
Pair each size 6 (4mm) and size 7 (4½mm) knitting needles

gauge

18 sts and 24 rows to 4in/10cm square over st st using size 7 (4½mm) needles.

abbreviations

beg = beginning

cm = centimeters

cont = continue

dec = decreas(e)ing

foll = following

in = inches

inc = increas(e)ing

k = knit

p = purl

rem = remain(ing)

St st = stockinette stitch

st(s) = stitch(es)

back and front
With size 7 (4½mm) needles, cast on 66(74:82) sts.

Beg with a k row, work 6 rows in St st.

Next row K2, [p2, k2] to end.

Next row P2, [k2, p2] to end.

Rep the last 2 rows once more.

Beg with a k row, work in st st until back/front measures 12¼(13¼:15)in/ 31(34:38)cm from cast-on edge, ending with a wrong side row.

Shape neck

Next row K24(27:30) sts, turn and work on these sts for first side of neck, leave rem sts on a spare needle.

Dec one st at neck edge of next 6 rows.

Work 3 rows.

Bind off.

With right side facing, slip center 18(20:22) sts onto a holder, rejoin yarn to rem sts, k to end.

Dec one st at neck edge of next 6 rows.

Work 3 rows.

Bind off.

sleeves   With size 6 (4mm) needles, cast on 34(38:42) sts.

Beg with a k row, work 6 rows St st.

Next row K2, [p2, k2] to end.

Next row P2, [k2, p2] to end.

Rep the last 2 rows once more.

Change to size 7 (4½mm) needles.

Beg with a k row, work in St st and inc one st at each end of the 3rd and every foll 4th row until there are 50(58:66) sts.

Work even until sleeve measures 7¾ (9:10¼)in/20(23:26)cm from cast-on edge, ending with a p row.

Next row K2, [p2, k2] to end.

Next row P2, [k2, p2] to end.

Rep the last 2 rows once more.

Bind off.

neckband   Join right shoulder seam.

With right side facing and size 7 (4½mm) needles, pick up and k 10 sts down left front neck, k across 18(20:22) sts from front neck holder, pick up and k 9 sts up right front neck and 9 sts down right back neck, k across 18(20:22) sts from back neck holder, then pick up and k 10 sts up left back neck. 74(78:82) sts.

Next row K2, [p2, k2] to end.

Next row P2, [k2, p2] to end.

Rep the last 2 rows once more.

Beg with a p row, work 5 rows St st.

Bind off.

to finish   Join left shoulder and neckband seam. With center of bound-off edge of sleeve to shoulder, sew on sleeves. Join side and sleeve seams.

cushion with denim ties

A simple stockinette stitch cushion in a crisp white cotton is embellished with fabric

bows made from soft, jeans-look fabric.

size
Approximately 16in/40cm square.

materials
Six 50g balls of Debbie Bliss cotton dk
in White
Pair size 6 (4mm) knitting needles
16in/40cm square pillow form
Strips of washed denim fabric

gauge
20 sts and 28 rows to 4in/10cm square over
St st using size 6 (4mm) needles.

abbreviations
beg = beginning
cm = centimeters
cont = continue
in = inches
k = knit
St st = stockinette stitch
st(s) = stitch(es)

to make
With size 6 (4mm) needles, cast on 83 sts.
K 3 rows.
Beg with a k row, work 9¾in/25cm in St st, ending with a k row.
Ridge row (wrong side) Knit.
Beg with a k row, cont in St st and work a further 16in/40cm, ending with a
k row.
Ridge row (wrong side) Knit.
Beg with a k row, cont in St st and work a further 9½in/24cm, ending with a
k row.
K 2 rows.
Bind off knitwise.

to finish
Fold the cushion cover in three along the ridge rows, with the cast-on and
bound-off edges overlapping to form the opening for the cushion back. Join the
side seams and insert the pillow form. Thread 5in/13cm lengths of denim
through the cushion front and tie.

floor cushions

These floor cushions are perfect for creating a relaxed, comfortable atmosphere.

They are inspired by stitch patterning on classic fishermen's sweaters.

garter stitch detail floor cushion

size
Approximately 25½in/65cm square.

materials
Seven 50g balls of Debbie Bliss cotton dk
in Navy
Pair size 6 (4mm) knitting needles
26 x 27½in/66 x 70cm fabric for cushion back
50cm/20in zipper
26–28in/66–70cm square pillow form

gauge
18 sts and 28 rows to 4in/10cm square over
patt using size 6 (4mm) needles.

abbreviations
cm = centimeters
in = inches
k = knit
p = purl
patt = pattern
rep = repeat
st(s) = stitch(es)

cushion front	With size 6 (4mm) needles, cast on 117 sts. **1st row** (right side) K5, [p3, k5] to end. **2nd row** Purl. Rep these 2 rows until cushion front measures 25½in/65cm from cast-on edge, ending with a right side row. Bind off.
cushion back	Cut two 26 x 13¾in/66 x 35cm pieces of fabric. With right sides together, pin and baste the two pieces together along one long edge, taking a ¾in/2cm seam. Remove pins and machine stitch for 3¼in/8cm at each end of the seam, leaving the center 20in/50cm unstitched for zipper placement. Press seam open. Lay zipper face down on the wrong side of the pressed seam and baste in place. From the right side, topstitch the zipper in place. Remove all the basting.
to finish	Open the zipper slightly and, with right sides together, lay the knitted cushion front on the cushion back and stitch around the edge. Open the zipper, turn right side out, and insert pillow form. Close zipper.

Guernsey floor cushion

size
Approximately 25½in/65cm square.

materials
Eight 50g balls of Debbie Bliss cotton dk in
Pale Blue
Pair size 6 (4mm) knitting needles
26 x 27½in/66 x 70cm fabric for cushion back
20in/50cm zipper
26–28in/66–70cm square pillow form

gauge
20 sts and 28 rows to 4in/10cm square over
St st using size 6 (4mm) needles.

abbreviations
beg = beginning
C4F = slip next 2 sts onto a cable needle and
hold at front of work, k2, then k2 from cable
needle
cm = centimeters
dec = decreas(e)ing
in = inches
k = knit
p = purl
patt = pattern
St st = stockinette stitch
st(s) = stitch(es)

pattern panel A (worked over 15 sts)

1st row (right side) K1, p13, k1.

2nd row P1, k13, p1.

3rd row As 1st row.

4th row P15.

5th row K15.

6th row P7, k1, p7.

7th row K6, p1, k1, p1, k6.

8th row P5, k1, p3, k1, p5.

9th row K4, p1, [k2, p1] twice, k4.

10th row P3, k1, p2, k1, p1, k1, p2, k1, p3.

11th row [K2, p1] twice, k3, [p1, k2] twice.

12th row P4, k1, [p2, k1] twice, p4.

13th row K3, p1, k2, p1, k1, p1, k2, p1, k3.

14th row As 8th row.

15th row As 9th row.

16th row P6, k1, p1, k1, p6.

17th row K5, p1, k3, p1, k5.

18th row As 6th row.

19th row K6, p3, k6.

20th row As 6th row.

21st row As 5th row.

22nd row As 4th row.

These 22 rows form Patt Panel A.

pattern panel B (worked over 13 sts)

1st row (right side) K1, p11, k1.

2nd row P1, k11, p1.

3rd row As 1st row.

4th row P13.

5th row K13.

6th row P6, k1, p6.

7th row K5, p1, k1, p1, k5.

8th row P4, k1, [p1, k1] twice, p4.

9th row K3, p1, [k1, p1] 3 times, k3.

10th row P2, k1, [p1, k1] 4 times, p2.

11th row K1, [p1, k1] 6 times.

12th row As 10th row.

13th row As 9th row.

14th row As 8th row.

15th row As 7th row.

16th row As 6th row.

17th row As 5th row.

18th row As 4th row.

These 18 rows form Patt Panel B.

pattern panel C (worked over 9 sts)

1st row (right side) K1, p7, k1.

2nd row P1, k7, p1.

3rd row As 1st row.

4th row P5, k2, p2.

5th row K3, p2, k4.

6th row P3, k2, p4.

7th row K5, p2, k2.

8th row P1, k2, p6.

9th row K6, p2, k1.

10th row P2, k2, p5.

11th row K4, p2, k3.

12th row P4, k2, p3.

13th row K2, p2, k5.

14th row P6, k2, p1.

15th row K1, p2, k6.

The 4th to 15th rows form Patt Panel C.

pattern panel D (worked over 4 sts)

1st row K4.

2nd row P4.

3rd row C4F.

4th row P4.

5th and 6th rows As 1st and 2nd rows.

These 6 rows form Patt Panel D.

cushion front

With size 6 (4mm) needles, cast on 118 sts.

Beg with a k row, work 6¾in/17cm in St st, ending with a p row and inc 9 sts evenly across last row. 127 sts.

Now work in patt as follows:

1st row (right side) P1, k1, p1, work across 1st row Patt Panel A, p1, k1, p1, work across 1st row Patt Panel B, p1, k1, p1, work across 1st row Patt Panel C, p1, k1, p1, work across 1st row Patt Panel D, p1, k1, p1, work across 1st row Patt Panel A, p1, k1, p1, work across 1st row Patt Panel D, p1, k1, p1, work across 1st row Patt Panel C, p1, k1, p1, work across 1st row Patt Panel B, p1, k1, p1, work across 1st row Patt Panel A, p1, k1, p1.

This row sets the position of the patt panels with 3 seed sts between each panel.

Cont in patt as set, working correct patt panel rows, until 6 repeats of Patt Panel A have been worked, so ending with a wrong side row.

Next row (right side) P and dec 9 sts evenly across row.

Next row Knit.

Next 2 rows Purl.

Next 2 rows Knit.

Next row Purl.

Next 2 rows Knit.

Next row Purl.

Next row Knit.

Next row Purl.

Bind off.

cushion back   Cut two 26 x 13¾in/66 x 35cm pieces of fabric. With right sides together, pin and tack-stitch the two pieces together along one long edge, taking a ¾in/2cm seam. Remove pins and machine stitch for 3¼in/8cm at each end of the seam, leaving the center 20in/50cm unstitched for zipper placement. Press seam open. Lay zipper face down on the wrong side of the pressed seam and baste in place. From the right side, topstitch the zipper in place. Remove all the basting.

to finish   Open the zipper slightly and, with right sides together, lay the knitted cushion front on the cushion back and stitch around the edge. Open the zipper, turn right side out and insert pillow form. Close zipper.

clothespin bag

A lining made from a bright and cheerful spotty fabric contrasts with the texture of

this practical seed stitch clothespin bag.

size
Approximately 10 x 12in/26 x 30cm.

materials
Three 50g balls of Debbie Bliss cotton dk
in White
Pair size 6 (4mm) knitting needles
13 x 21¾in/34 x 55cm piece of fabric for lining
Sewing thread
12in/30cm plain wooden coat hanger

gauge
20 sts and 33 rows to 4in/10cm square over
seed st using size 6 (4mm) needles.

abbreviations
cm = centimeters
in = inches
k = knit
p = purl
st(s) = stitch(es)

to make With size 6 (4mm) needles, cast on 61 sts.

Seed st row K1, [p1, k1] to end.

This row forms seed st and is repeated throughout.

Work in seed st for 18in/46cm, ending with a right side row.

Next row Seed st 16, bind off next 29 sts knitwise, seed st to end.

Next row Work in seed st and cast on 29 sts over bound-off sts of previous row.

Work a further 2½in/6cm in seed st, ending with a right side row.

Bind off knitwise.

Fold in half and join side seams.

lining   Fold lining fabric in half widthwise, then, taking a ⅝in/1½cm allowance, join the seam for 3¾in/9½cm at each end, leaving a central 6in/15cm gap. Press seam open. Refold so that seam is placed 2¼in/6cm below top fold. Press along folds. Taking ⅝in/1½cm seams, join one side seam for the full length and then join the other side seam leaving a gap in the seam just large enough to insert the hanger. Make a small hole in the center of the top fold for the hanger hook and insert the hanger. Close gap in side seam. Insert lining with hanger into the knitted section and join the top seam on each side of the hook. Slip stitch lining to knitting around front opening.

seed stitch blanket

A cotton denim-style yarn used double creates a soft but sturdy fabric, which is perfect for a beach blanket.

size
28½ x 36in/72.5 x 92cm.

materials
Seventeen 50g balls of Debbie Bliss cotton denim aran in Medium Blue
Pair size 10½ (7mm) knitting needles

gauge
12 sts and 21 rows to 4in/10cm square over seed st using size 10½ (7mm) needles and two strands of yarn held together.

abbreviations
cm = centimeters
in = inches
k = knit
p = purl
st(s) = stitch(es)

to make With size 10½ (7mm) needles and two strands of yarn held together, cast on 87 sts.
Seed st row K1, [p1, k1] to end.
This row forms seed st and is repeated throughout.
Work in seed st until blanket measures 36in/92cm.
Bind off in seed st.
Darn in all yarn ends.

seaside throw

Here is a throw that uses traditional Guernsey patterns with lace and bobbles. The cotton yarn gives clarity to the stitch detail.

size
Approximately 35½in x 51¼in/90 x 130cm.

materials
Twenty-one 50g balls of Debbie Bliss cotton dk in Pale Blue
Pair each size 5 (3¾mm) and size 6 (4mm) knitting needles

gauge
20 sts and 28 rows to 4in/10cm square over St st using size 6 (4mm) needles.

abbreviations
beg = beginning
C4F = slip next 2 sts onto cable needle and hold at front of work, k2, then k2 from cable needle
cm = centimeters
in = inches
k = knit
mb = knit into front and back of next stitch twice, then pass 3rd, 2nd and 1st sts over 4th st, so making bobble
p = purl
patt = pattern
pfb = purl into front and back of next st
rep = repeat
skp = slip 1, knit 1, pass slipped stitch over
st st = stocking stitch
st(s) = stitch(es)
tog = together
yo = yarn over

pattern
panel A
(worked
over 4 sts)

1st row (right side) K4.

2nd row P4.

3rd and 4th rows As 1st and 2nd rows.

5th row C4F.

6th row P4.

These 6 rows form Patt Panel A.

pattern
panel B
(worked
over 11 sts)

1st row (right side) K11.

2nd row P11.

3rd row K5, p1, k5.

4th row P4, k1, p1, k1, p4.

5th row K3, [p1, k1] twice, p1, k3.

6th row P2, [k1, p1] 3 times, k1, p2.

7th row K1, [p1, k1] 4 times, p1, k1.

8th row As 6th row.

9th row As 5th row.

10th row As 4th row.

11th row As 3rd row.

12th row As 2nd row

13th to 16th rows K11.

These 16 rows form Patt Panel B.

pattern
panel C
(worked
over 11 sts)

1st row (right side) K5, yo, skp, k4.

2nd and every wrong side row P11.

3rd row K3, k2tog, yo, k1, yo, skp, k3.

5th row K2, k2tog, yo, k3, yo, skp, k2.

7th row K1, k2tog, yo, k2, mb, k2, yo, skp, k1.

8th row P11.

These 8 rows form Patt Panel C.

to make With size 5 (3¾mm) needles, cast on 168 sts.

1st row (right side) [K1, p1] to end.

2nd row [P1, k1] to end.

3rd to 7th rows Rep 1st and 2nd rows twice more, then 1st row again.

Inc row (wrong side) Seed st 5, [pfb, pfb, seed st 37] 4 times, pfb, pfb, seed st 5. 178 sts.

Change to size 6 (4mm) needles.

Now work in pattern as follows:

1st row (right side) Seed st 5, [work 1st row Patt Panel A, seed st 5, work 1st row Patt Panel B, seed st 5, work 1st row Patt Panel C, seed st 5] 4 times, work 1st row Patt Panel A, seed st 5.

2nd row Seed st 5, [work 2nd row Patt Panel A, seed st 5, work 2nd row Patt Panel C, seed st 5, work 2nd row Patt Panel B, seed st 5] 4 times, work 2nd row Patt Panel A, seed st 5.

These 2 rows set the position of the pattern panels with seed st between.

Cont in patt until work measures approximately 50½in/128cm from beg, ending with a 12th row of Patt Panel B.

Change to size 5 (3¾mm) needles.

Dec row (right side) Seed st 5, [work 2tog, work 2tog, seed st 37] 4 times, k2tog, p2tog, seed st 5. 168 sts.

Work 7 rows in seed st.

Bind off.

tote bag

What a great bag for the beach or picnics. This one is large enough to contain your
favorite book, sunglasses, and lunch. An additional pocket on the outside can house
your cell phone, too.

size
Approximately 14½ x 8¾in/37 x 22cm.

materials
Six 50g balls of Debbie Bliss cotton dk
in White
Pair size 6 (4mm) knitting needles
One size 6 (4mm) circular needle
½yd/50cm of 44in/112cm wide fabric for lining

gauge
20 sts and 28 rows to 4in/10cm square over
St st using size 6 (4mm) needles.

abbreviations
cm = centimeters

cont = continue

in = inches

inc = increas(e)ing

k = knit

kfb = k into front and back of st

p = purl

rep = repeat

sl = slip

St st = stockinette stitch

st(s) = stitch(es)

tog = together

yo = yarn over

pocket lining
With size 6 (4mm) needles, cast on 21 sts.
Beg with a k row, work 26 rows in St st.
Leave sts on a holder.

base
With size 6 (4mm) circular needle, cast on 5 sts.
1st row (right side) [Kfb] 4 times, k1. 9 sts.
2nd and all wrong side rows Purl.
3rd row [Kfb] 8 times, k1. 17 sts.
5th row [K1, kfb] 8 times, k1. 25 sts.
7th row [K2, kfb] 8 times, k1. 33 sts.
9th row [K3, kfb] 8 times, k1. 41 sts.
Cont to work in St st and inc 8 sts across every right side row as set, working one st more before each inc as set until there are 137 sts, ending with a right side row.

main bag
Ridge row (wrong side) Knit.
Next row Knit.
Next 2 rows K1, [p1, k1] to end.
Next row *K1, [p1, k1] 3 times, p3; rep from * to last 7 sts, [k1, p1] 3 times, k1.
Next row K1, *[p1, k1] twice, p1, k5; rep from * to last 6 sts, [p1, k1] 3 times.
Next row P2, *k1, p1, k1, p7; rep from * to last 5 sts, k1, p1, k1, p2.
Next row K3, *p1, k9; rep from * to last 4 sts, p1, k3.
Beg with a p row, work even in St st until work measures 10¾in/27cm from ridge row, ending with a p row.
Place pocket
Next row K58, sl next 21 sts onto a holder, k across 21 sts from pocket lining, k to end.
Cont in St st until work measures 13¾in/35cm from ridge row, ending with a p row.
Next row (right side) K3, *p1, k9; rep from * to last 4 sts, p1, k3.
Next row P2, *k1, p1, k1, p7; rep from * to last 5 sts, k1, p1, k1, p2.
Next row K1, *[p1, k1] twice, p1, k5; rep from * to last 6 sts, [p1, k1] 3 times.

Next row *K1, [p1, k1] 3 times, p3; rep from * to last 7 sts, [k1, p1] 3 times, k1.

Next 2 rows K1, [p1, k1] to end.

K 1 row.

P 1 row.

Eyelet row (right side) K4, yo, k2tog, k to last 6 sts, k2tog, yo, k4.

P 1 row.

K 1 row.

Ridge row (wrong side) Knit.

Beg with a p row, work 4 rows.

Bind off.

pocket top

With right side facing and size 6 (4mm) needles, work across 21 sts from pocket holder as follows:

Seed st row K1, [p1, k1] to end.

Rep this row 4 times more.

Bind off knitwise.

to finish

Stitch pocket lining and edges of pocket top in place. Join seam in base and cont to bound-off edge. Fold top over onto wrong side along ridge row and slip stitch the hem in place. Make a braid approximately 51in/130cm long from 6 strands of yarn, tie each end of the braid and thread through the top hem from one eyelet to the other. Tie together the ends of the braid.

lining

Cut a 8¾in/22cm circle from strong cardboard (use a plate or bowl to draw around) for the base. Using the cardboard base as a template, cut a circle from the lining fabric allowing an extra ⅝in/1½cm all around. Place cardboard base into the knitted bag. Cut a 28¼ x 15¼in/72 x 39cm piece of fabric, fold in half, and stitch into a tube along the shorter sides, taking a ⅝in/1½cm seam. Stitch circular fabric base into one end of the tube. Press a ⅝in/1½cm hem onto the wrong side of the open end, insert into the knitted bag, aligning the seams, and slip stitch around the top.

yarn distributors

For Debbie Bliss yarn supplier information only, please contact:

USA
Knitting Fever, Inc.
P.O. Box 336
315 Bayview Avenue
Amityville, NY 11701

Tel: (516) 546-3600
www.knittingfever.com
e-mail:
knittingfever@knittingfever.com

CANADA
Diamond Yarns Ltd.
155 Martin Ross Avenue Unit 3
Toronto
Ontario M3J 2L9
Canada

Tel: 001 416 736 6111
www.diamondyarn.com

AUSTRALIA
Jo Sharp Pty Ltd.
P.O. Box 1018
Fremantle
WA 6959
Australia

Tel: +61 (0)8 9430 9699
e-mail: yarn@josharp.com.au

BELGIUM/HOLLAND
Pavan
Meerlaanstraat 73
Oostrezele 9860
Belgium

Tel: +32 9221 8594
Fax +32 9221 5662
e-mail: pavan@pandora.be

FRANCE
Elle Tricote
8 Rue du Coq
La Petit France
67000 Strasbourg
France

Tel: +33 (0)388 230313
www.elletricote.com.fr

**GERMANY/AUSTRIA/
SWITZERLAND**
Designer Yarns
Handelsagentur Klaus Koch
Mauritius Str, 130
50226 Frechen
Germany

Tel: +49 (0) 2234 205453
Fax: +49 2234 205456
www.designeryarns.de

JAPAN
Eisaku Noro & Co. Ltd.
55 Shimoda Ohibino Azaichou
Ichinomita Aichi
4910105
Japan

Tel: +81 52 203 5100
www.eisakunoro.com

MEXICO
Red Color S.A. DE CV
San Antonio 105
Col. Santa Maria
Monterrey
N.L. 64650
Mexico

Tel: +52 818 173 3700
e-mail: Abremer@starsoft.co.mx

SPAIN
Oyambre
Pau Claris 145
08009 Barcelona
Spain

Tel: +34 934 872672
e-mail: oyambre@oyambreonline.
com

SWEDEN
Hamilton Design
Långgatan 20
SE-64730 Mariefred
Sweden

Tel: +46 (0)159 12006
www.hamiltondesign.biz

UK
Designer Yarns Ltd.
Units 8-10 Newbridge Industrial
Estate
Pitt Street
Keighley
W. Yorkshire BD21 4PQ
UK

Tel: +44 (0)1535 664222
Fax: +44 (01535) 664333
www.designeryarns.uk.com
e-mail: jane@designeryarns.uk.com

For information about Debbie Bliss products and Debbie Bliss *the club*, visit www.debbieblissonline.com

acknowledgments

This book would not have been possible without the invaluable contribution of the following people:

Rosy Tucker, for both her invaluable creative and practical collaboration and her support on this book, including the pattern checking.

Penny Hill, for pattern compiling and for organizing her great team of knitters.

Pia Tryde, the photographer, and Julia Bird, the stylist, who created the beautiful look and feel of the book and who, together with Marco, the assistant, made the shoot such a joy to work on.

Sarah Lavelle and Carey Smith at Ebury, for their support and for making the book happen.

Christine Wood, for her great book design.

The wonderful knitters, without whom none of this would have happened: Cynthia Brent, Pat Church, Jacqui Dunt, Penny Hill, Maisie Lawrence, Frances Wallace.

Emma Callery, a perfect and unflappable editor.

Heather Jeeves, my wonderful agent.

The models, Evie, Jo, Madeleine, and Rose.

The knitters, retailers, and distributors who support my books and yarns.

Thank you to Cath Kidston for the use of her products in the book and to Melanie and Tom Petherick for the use of their beautiful seaside home.